W9-AHG-898

J1

PARROTS

LIVING WILD

LIVING WILD

Published by Creative Education

P.O. Box 227, Mankato, Minnesota 56002

Creative Education is an imprint of The Creative Company

Design and production by Mary Herrmann

Art direction by Rita Marshall

Printed in the United States of America

Photographs by Getty Images (Theo Allofs, Tui De Roy, Tim Flach, Rene Frederick, Darrell Gulin, August Macke, Claus Meyer, Pete Oxford, Stuart Westmorland, Art Wolfe), iStockphoto (Les Cunliffe, Shuvabrata Deb, Rebecca Dickerson, Jeremy Edwards, Lee Feldstein, Susan Flashman, Steffen Foerster, Aleksejs Jevsejenko, Goran Kapor, Kateryna, Valerie Loiseleux, Lori Martin, Chad McDermott, Brent Melton, Jason Meyer, Zeynep Mufti, Govert Nieuwland, Brian Owens, Michael Price, Carlos Restrepo, Roberto A Sanchez, Olga Solovei, Michael Willis)

Library of Congress Cataloging-in-Publication Data

Hanel, Rachael.

Parrots / by Rachael Hanel.

p. cm. — (Living wild)

Includes index.

ISBN 978-1-58341-657-0

1. Parrots—Juvenile literature. I. Title. II. Series.

QL696.P7H36 2008

598.7'1—dc22   2007019628

First Edition

9 8 7 6 5 4 3 2 1

CREATIVE EDUCATION

PARROTS

Rachael Hanel

As the sun edges slowly over the
horizon, a group of scarlet macaws

that had been dozing through
the night starts to awaken.

As the sun edges slowly over the horizon, a group of scarlet macaws that had been dozing through the night starts to awaken. The brightly colored birds perch high in the trees of the Brazilian forest. As the sunlight becomes stronger, the macaws become more active. The dozen or so birds squawk loudly to each other, and soon, they lift up together in flight. Their wings are a blur

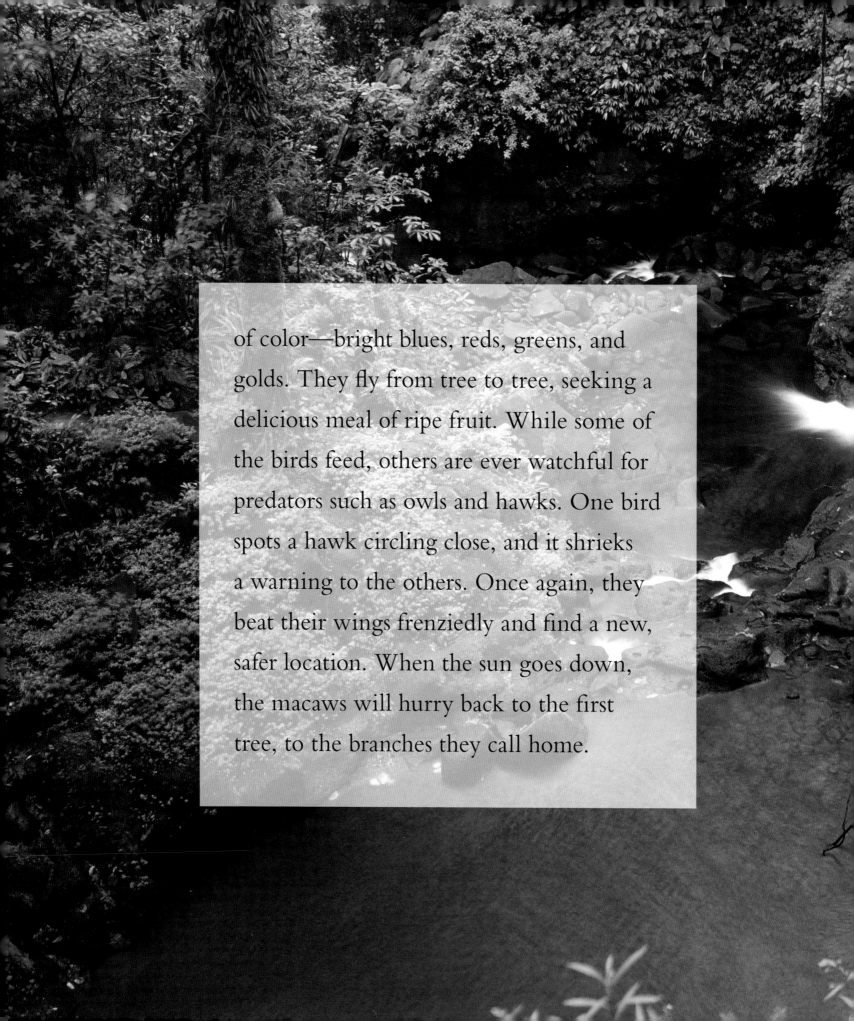

of color—bright blues, reds, greens, and golds. They fly from tree to tree, seeking a delicious meal of ripe fruit. While some of the birds feed, others are ever watchful for predators such as owls and hawks. One bird spots a hawk circling close, and it shrieks a warning to the others. Once again, they beat their wings frenziedly and find a new, safer location. When the sun goes down, the macaws will hurry back to the first tree, to the branches they call home.

WHERE IN THE WORLD THEY LIVE

■ **African Grey Parrot**
rainforests of West
and Central Africa

■ **Scarlet Macaw**
Central America,
northern half of
South America

■ **Orange-billed
Lorikeet**
Indonesia

■ **Budgerigar**
Australia

■ **Eclectus Parrot**
New Guinea

Wild parrots are found primarily in Africa, Asia,
Australia, and South America but also appear in certain
other areas of the world. The 333 species are widely
distributed and too numerous to be shown here. The
colored dots instead represent the habitats of five of
the most well-known and distinctive species.

A DIVERSE GROUP

The parrot, with its splendid and varied colors, is one of the most beautiful birds in the world. For centuries, its bright **plumage** and ability to **mimic** sounds have made it an object of curiosity as well as a sought-after pet in many households.

There are more than 300 kinds of parrots in the world today. The parrot family, Psittacidae, is split into 85 groups called genera. Each genus can contain several species. Included in the parrot family are such birds as macaws, parakeets, lorikeets, lovebirds, and kakapos. Close relatives of the parrot include cockatoos, cockatiels, pigeons, cuckoos, swifts, and owls.

Parrots live in many different habitats throughout Africa, Asia, Australia, and South America. They can also be found in Central America, and some birds will occasionally migrate into the extreme southwestern United States. **Feral** populations of parrots, many of which are abandoned pets and their descendants, exist in large cities such as San Francisco and New York City.

Many parrots call the tropical forested regions of South America, southern Asia, and central Africa home. In

The rainbow lorikeet is one of 53 colorful species of lorikeet found in Australia and New Guinea.

such places, daytime temperatures are consistently warm, ranging from 82 to 86 °F (28 to 30 °C), and temperatures rarely drop below 68 °F (20 °C) at night. The large, leafy trees of tropical forests provide ready food such as fruit, nuts, seeds, and berries.

Some parrots are found in the drier regions of central Africa, central Asia, and Australia. These areas have fewer trees than the rainforests, and parrots live in shorter trees and low-lying bushes called shrubs. Here, temperatures range widely, reaching highs of more than 100 °F (40 °C) during the day and plummeting to 50 °F (10 °C) in the evening. Some parrots, such as the budgerigar in Australia, can survive in desert environments; others, like the orange-billed lorikeet, can live in mountains. A few species—such as the night parrot, ground parrot, and red-fronted parakeet—live in open areas on the plains with no trees whatsoever.

Every parrot, no matter its genus or species, possesses a body that is made for flying, climbing trees, and finding food. All parrots share certain physical characteristics such as a large head, short neck, and small curved beak. Like most flying birds, their skeletons are made of hollow

Many parrots are at home in the tropical forests (opposite) of the world.

Parrots bathe infrequently. They rely on preening to stay clean, soak in the occasional rain shower, or flap their wings on wet tree leaves.

Parrots' beaks can be different sizes and colors, but they all have the same basic shape.

Parrots will drink once a day on average. Species that eat juicy fruits need to drink less often than those that eat dry seeds.

bones, which make the birds light and able to fly. On their zygodactyl feet, two claws point forward, and two point back, which helps parrots climb trees and rocky outcroppings.

The strong claws serve different functions. Most other birds' feet have three claws that point forward and one that points back. But because parrots are zygodactyl, they are better able to climb and cling to tree branches. A parrot often acts like a tiny acrobat, hanging upside down from a branch to reach food. When it walks on a branch, it slowly inches its feet sideways. Parrots also use their feet to **preen** themselves and to pick up food.

All parrots have a strong, rounded bill, with the upper **mandible** fitting precisely over the lower mandible. The upper mandible curves down, while the lower mandible curves up. The beak's sharp points help the bird crack open hard food, such as nuts and seeds. A hinge on the bill gives the parrot leverage when crunching its food. The beak is also sometimes used as an extra foot in climbing.

A parrot's eyesight and hearing are particularly sharp. It has the ability to see colors and will usually pick bright,

A parrot's claws help it grip food such as fruit in a similar way as humans use their fingers.

ripe fruit to eat over duller, unripe fruit. It can focus its
vision at both long and short distances. A parrot's ears,
even though they are internal and cannot be seen, can
detect a wide range of sounds, both low and high. The
tongue of a parrot is thick and flexible, which allows it to
feel its food and could be one reason that parrots are able
to mimic the sounds they hear.

Parrots have two types of feathers. The outer ones
are called contour feathers and overlap like roof shingles.
Closer to the skin is a layer of down. This helps protect
the bird's sensitive skin from harsh elements such as wind
and rain. The density of a parrot's down and contour

feathers depends upon where the bird lives. In cooler climates, the feathers are packed tightly together to retain heat. In tropical climates, feathers are spaced farther apart. This allows air to flow through and ruffle the feathers, which helps keep a parrot cool. On most parrots' tails, 12 feathers are arranged in a semicircular pattern.

The sheer number of parrots makes for a variety of physical differences among the species. The major differences among parrots are in their sizes, wing shapes, and colors. The largest member of the parrot family is the macaw, which is native to the rainforests of South and Central America. Macaws can grow up to 39 inches

The spread-apart feathers of a blue and gold macaw indicate that it lives in a warmer climate.

Rather than fly, the rotund kakapo waddles like a duck.

The New Zealand kakapo is the only parrot that cannot fly. For this reason, it was easy prey for predators and is now found only in designated havens.

(1 m) from head to tail and weigh nearly 4 pounds (1.8 kg). The rotund kakapo, a flightless parrot of New Zealand, can weigh up to six and a half pounds (3 kg). The smallest parrot, the pygmy parrot, lives in New Guinea and the surrounding islands. It is the size of a sparrow, reaching a height of only about four inches (10 cm) and weighing one-third of an ounce (10 g).

Parrots that fly often, such as those that live in dry grasslands with few trees, have narrow wings and long tails that give them the ability to travel faster and for longer distances. Parrots that climb and fly mostly short distances, such as those that live in dense rainforests, sport rounded, broad wings and short tails.

Almost every color is represented among parrots. The most common parrot color is green, but some display a mixture of colors. The most brightly colored birds live in rainforests and are splashed with streaks of blue, red, yellow, and green. These colors help **camouflage** a parrot as it flies from branch to branch amid the equally colorful tropical forests. Parrots that live in drier regions, such as grasslands and deserts, do not possess such bright feathers. Each parrot's plumage blends into its surroundings.

Unlike most birds, scarlet macaws of both sexes have the same brilliant coloring.

Hyacinth macaws have incredibly strong beaks that can crack coconuts and macadamia nuts.

FAMILY LIFE

P arrots spend their active lives flitting from branch to branch. They are social creatures and live together in groups called flocks. Some flocks consist of hundreds of birds, while other flocks may have as few as 20 members.

Parrots start their days together, waking up before dawn in a central sleeping location. They leave their **roosts** at sunrise to look for food. How far they fly depends upon how many trees with sufficient food are nearby. In tropical areas where food is plentiful, parrots do not have to travel far. Instead, they rely more on their climbing skills to reach food higher up in the tall trees and plants. But in drier regions where trees and shrubs are widely scattered, parrots may have to fly many miles a day.

Parrots remain quiet during the heat of the day and return to their roosts to rest. In the hour or two before sunset, they become active and feed again. When the sun sets, they go back to their central location to sleep, staying quiet, and thus protected, through the night.

Parrots eat nuts, berries, grains, fruits, insects, and worms. They like to take their time eating and often

Some parrots' coloring helps them blend in with their leafy surroundings.

Like humans, parrots favor a dominant side of their bodies and can be considered "right-footed" or "left-footed."

A parrot's head can turn only so far to help it clean its many feathers.

Parrots partake in allopreening, in which partners preen and clean each other. This helps to strengthen the bond between partners.

will turn the food over and over in their feet to look at, smell, and, finally, taste it. They like food that is colorful, flavorful, and full of texture because of their keen senses of sight and taste. When parrots eat seeds, they use the tips of their bills to break open the seed or shell, or they press it against the roof of their mouths with their tongues.

Parrots spend a large portion of each day caring for their feathers. Several times a day, a parrot will clean itself. To do this, a parrot rakes its bill through the feathers one by one. Parrots have flexible necks and can twist their heads nearly all the way around their bodies in order to reach their wing and tail feathers. Parrots cannot reach the feathers on their heads or throats with their bills, so they use their claws to scratch those parts of their bodies. To keep their bills and claws sharp and clean, parrots scrape them against rough surfaces, such as tree bark. After they clean their plumage, or after they've slept, parrots raise all their feathers as high as they can and give a good shake.

A parrot loses its feathers once a year in a process called molting, which usually occurs after the breeding season. During molting, a parrot's old feathers fall out as new ones grow in. Molting is naturally **staggered** so the parrot

always has enough feathers for flying and insulation, but the entire process can take several weeks.

When it is time to mate, a season that varies among parrot species, the birds seek out their partners from previous years. Parrots generally keep the same mate for life. To create a nest, both the male and female find a hole in a tree. They prefer small holes—ones that are often just big enough for their bodies to slip into. They enlarge an existing hole with their beak and use the resulting wood chips, along with feathers and leaves,

Preening is a social activity for many parrots.

If parrots do not live in forests where trees are readily available for nesting, they often use bushes.

to create a cozy spot. Parrots often return to the same breeding location every year.

After mating, the female bird lays two to five eggs, usually over the course of several days. The female **incubates** the group of eggs, called a clutch, while the male searches for food and brings it back to the nest. Because the eggs are laid at different times, chicks usually hatch in one- or two-day intervals. Parrot chicks are tiny, blind, helpless creatures when they make their way out of their shells using their beaks. Many species do not have feathers when they are born, though some, such as the African grey, are born with a downy coat. The mother stays with the chicks for the first few days, while the father leaves to find food. The father comes back to the nest and gives food to the mother, who then eats it and feeds the chicks **regurgitated** morsels. After a week or so, the mother also leaves the chicks to find food.

Once the chicks' feathers start coming in after a couple of weeks, they are able to eat on their own. They leave the nest to learn how to fly, but they continue to stay close to their parents. They watch and learn essential

survival skills, such as how to avoid predators, how to find food, and how to interact in a large group.

Parrots do not breed until they are three to five years old. Up until that time, they live with the flock, and all the young birds stick together. The youngsters form friendships and may even start choosing their mates, even though they are too young to breed. Parrots are loyal partners. Even outside of breeding season, adult pairs tend to stay together.

Parrots face many dangers when they are young. Chicks

that cannot yet fly are the most vulnerable, especially if they fall to the ground. Snakes, hawks, and wild cats like to prey upon parrots. But as the birds get older and fly, they find safety in numbers. In a flock, several parrots serve as designated "lookouts" and use their strong senses to notice predators. If parrots spot a predator, they call to the others in a series of sharp, shrill noises. When this occurs, all members of the flock take off and fly to a new location.

A parrot's most distinctive behavior is probably its ability to mimic sounds it hears. Parrots have been known to repeat words, animal sounds, or household noises such as doorbell rings. The African grey parrot is the best talker of them all. Since wild parrots do not normally encounter humans, they do not imitate human speech naturally. Instead, African greys most often imitate the sounds of other birds—or even bats.

Parrots can live for several years. Smaller parrot species can reach their teens, while larger parrots can live to be 25, 30, or even 40 years old or more. In rare cases, 80-year-old parrots—and some even upward of 100—have been reported in captivity.

Parrots are quick to take flight if they feel threatened by predators.

Parrots have been kept as pets for hundreds of years, but they were especially popular in 19th-century Europe.

A SOUGHT-AFTER TREASURE

P arrots and humans have had a long-standing relationship dating back many centuries. The ancient Egyptians revered parrots, which they took to be gods in animal form. **Hieroglyphics** that are more than 4,000 years old depict parrots, and mummified parrots have been found in Egyptian tombs. Parrots are also mentioned in anonymous writings from India and Persia (Iran) dating back 3,000 years.

Greek ruler Alexander the Great is thought to have introduced the parrot to Europe when he brought it back from his travels to India and Persia in the fourth century B.C. Ancient Romans and Greeks kept parrots in elaborate cages made of tortoise shell or ivory. The Romans established large **aviaries** and introduced the parrot throughout their vast empire, which comprised most of today's western Europe, northern Africa, and the Middle East.

Parrots quickly became a symbol of wealth throughout Europe because they were rare and expensive to obtain. However, the parrots' popularity soon made them vulnerable to extinction. They were captured in the wild

In 1493, explorer Christopher Columbus returned from South America with a pair of Cuban Amazon parrots as a gift for Queen Isabella of Spain.

to be used as pets, and they were also killed for their feathers and meat.

For centuries, parrot feathers have been used in ceremonial rituals among native tribes of the world, but this did not have a negative effect upon parrots' total numbers. But as world trade expanded in the 16th and 17th centuries, more parrots were captured so that their feathers could be given as gifts to explorers. The feathers became part of a larger global trade, and they decorated items such as women's clothes, purses, and hats. Many birds were killed to meet the demands of the wealthy, and 18 parrot species became extinct between 1600 and 1980.

The U.S. witnessed the demise of its only native parrot, the Carolina parakeet. Through the 19th century, this parrot could be found in the woods of the eastern and midwestern U.S., as far north as the Great Lakes region and as far west as Nebraska. As America became more populated in the 1800s, settlers cut down trees to clear land for homes, cities, and agriculture. Much of the Carolina parakeet's habitat was destroyed. In addition, the bird was shot by farmers, who considered the parrot a nuisance because it ate crops, and by traders, who sought

its colorful feathers. By 1860, the bird was rarely found outside of Florida, and by 1914, it had disappeared entirely.

Today, estimates vary as to how many parrot species are threatened. Organizations such as the World Conservation Union and Birds International conclude that anywhere between 25 and 35 percent of parrots are either near threatened or threatened enough to be considered endangered. The birds have faced the biggest threats from the destruction of habitat, harvesting for feathers, and their capture for the pet trade.

Still, the parrot is in great demand as a household pet, and overall, birds are the third-most popular pet behind cats and dogs. Because parrot populations are vulnerable, their trade is carefully regulated. According to the Convention on International Trade in Endangered Species

The Carolina parakeet was a conure like those pictured above; conures are a branch of American parrots.

People who keep parrots as pets need to be aware of the dangers that life in captivity poses to birds.

of Wild Fauna and Flora (CITES) treaty signed in 1973, 40 parrot species cannot be traded whatsoever because of their vulnerability and potential extinction. Most of the remaining species can be traded, but only with the use of strict permits and regulations. More than 160 countries agreed to follow CITES regulations.

Mortality rates for captured parrots vary widely, with anywhere from 5 to 60 percent dying before they can be traded. Trade most often threatens larger parrots such as macaws, because they do not produce offspring as often as smaller parrots. Therefore, their population in the wild grows slowly and is difficult to replenish.

In the U.S., the Wild Bird Conservation Act was adopted in 1992. The act bans the importation of most wild parrots except those from countries that have strong parrot management and conservation programs, or countries that breed their parrots in captivity rather than capture them in the wild. The U.S. imports about 17,000 parrots each year, and about one-fifth of those are taken from the wild. Today's stricter laws mean fewer wild birds are captured for trade, while more birds are being bred in captivity to supply the market.

Many U.S. presidents and first ladies, including John F. Kennedy, Teddy Roosevelt, Dolly Madison, and Martha Washington, have owned parrots.

In the eclectus parrot species, the male is predominantly green, while the female is red.

The popularity and novelty of parrots, which began several centuries ago, continues today in popular culture references. One of the most enduring images is of a parrot sitting on a pirate's shoulder. This image is based on the fact that pirates, who traveled the world in the 16th and 17th centuries, often came across the exotic birds while docked in tropical locations. Parrots likely provided amusement for pirates when they showed off their mimicry abilities. In addition, Europeans prized parrots, and pirates could make money by selling the creatures.

Robert Louis Stevenson, a 19th-century Scottish author, wrote about pirates in his 1883 novel *Treasure Island*. In the story, the pirate Long John Silver keeps a pet parrot, which he names Cap'n Flint. The pirate claims the bird is 200 years old and has traveled the world. Cap'n Flint echoes the words of the ship's crew and often cries out "Pieces of eight! Pieces of eight!" in reference to gold coins the pirates have captured.

Ovid, one of the greatest writers of the early Roman Empire, wrote a long poem called "On the Death of a Parrot" around 18 B.C. In the **elegy**, he asks other birds to mourn the pet, which had come all the way from India.

In the 1992 Walt Disney movie *Aladdin*, set in Arabia, the villain Jafar owns a parrot named Iago who is rude, selfish, and obnoxious. The evil pair kidnaps the hero Aladdin in hopes of gaining a magic lamp from the Cave of Wonders, but Aladdin eventually escapes. Iago and Jafar also play central roles in *The Return of Jafar, Aladdin*'s 1994 sequel. In this movie, Iago experiences a change of heart and leaves Jafar.

In *102 Dalmatians*, another Disney animated movie, a macaw named Waddlesworth believes he is a Rottweiler, not a parrot. He lives in a dog shelter and refuses to fly, because dogs can't fly. But in the end, he flies and acts more like a parrot while still declaring that he is a dog at heart.

In about one-third of all parrot species, the male and female sport different colors; the male is the more colorful of the two.

ELEGY VI:
ON THE DEATH OF A PARROT

There, in Elysium, on a hill-side's gentle slope there stands a forest of broad, shady oaks, and over the moist soil the rich grass spreads its coverlet of green. Here, if the fabled tale we may believe, abide all innocent birds, and here no fowl of evil omen ever comes. Here range the harmless swans, and here the one undying Phoenix dwells. Here doth the peacock proudly show his gorgeous plumage and the crooning dove showers kisses on her eager mate. Here in their midst, here in these pleasant woody places, our parrot speaks and calls around him all birds of gentle soul. His bones a mound doth cover, a little mound as doth befit his size, and on it is a little stone that bears this little legend:

From this memorial, you may see
What love my mistress bore to me.
Whene'er to her I spake, my words
Meant more than any other bird's.

Ovid (43 B.C.–A.D. 17),
excerpt from Amores

LEARNING MORE

T oday, when scientists devote time to the examination of parrots, they do so primarily by focusing on ways to rebuild or conserve parrot populations that are threatened or vulnerable. Research that closely examines habitat and the birds' relation to farmland can help reverse negative population trends.

Parrots have lived on Earth for millions of years. The oldest parrot-like fossil was found in Wyoming and dates back 65 to 74 million years ago. Even though parrots are not found in Europe today, two species that appear to be closely related to today's parrots have been identified from 40-million-year-old fossils uncovered in France. Parrots evolved in forests but have now adapted to man-made habitats as well. Many find food in cultivated farmlands, while others make their homes on abandoned coffee or rubber plantations.

Scientists and government officials in countries around the world are trying to find ways to restore parrot populations. For example, in Australia, scientists have been tracking the orange-bellied parrot for several years, since that species is considered critically endangered.

Hanging parrots get their name from their strange habit of roosting upside down from a branch. They are also known as "bat parrots."

Rainbow lorikeets, like lovebirds, are some of the least threatened species of parrots in the world.

Lovebirds are a type of parrot that received their name due to their uncommon faithfulness to their partners year after year.

For thousands of years, this parrot migrated from the island of Tasmania to the salt marshes and dunes of southern Australia to breed. Over the past 200 years, these breeding sites have been cleared to make way for human development. This interrupted the parrot's breeding habits, and its numbers plummeted. Today, members of the Orange-Bellied Parrot Recovery Team capture the parrots and breed them in captivity. They also focus on restoring the bird's habitat so the parrot can be reintroduced into the wild.

In many tropical forests where parrots are found in great numbers, intense logging activities have reduced the birds' habitat. The thick-billed parrot once lived in the mountainous regions of Mexico, and its range extended into Arizona and New Mexico. Reduction of habitat has restricted it to just the forested mountains of northern Mexico. Conservation officials estimate that only .06 percent of the bird's original forestland remains. Scientists regularly monitor nesting sites and try to create new ones. In some of the more popular nesting areas, money is given to Mexican tree farmers to leave trees where they are instead of cutting them down and selling them.

Other efforts to conserve parrot populations focus on helping farmers discourage parrots from feeding on crops. For years, as the traditional forest habitats of parrots have been replaced by farmland, farmers have considered parrots pests because they like to eat grains, which reduces harvests. In Australia, some experiments to keep parrots away from crops have met with success. For example, crops are planted so they grow at a time when the birds' migratory flight paths take them past farmland. Also, "decoy" crops are planted to protect the real crops. In some areas, nets placed over orchard trees prevent parrots from snacking on the fruit.

To help increase parrot populations in the wild, scientists try to create as many nesting sites as possible. Parrots like to nest in trees that become hollow due to age and disease. As more forests are cleared of dead and decaying trees, few nesting sites for parrots remain. It can take a tree up to 100 years to become hollow enough for a parrot to live in, so new trees that are planted now will not make good nests for several generations to come. Instead, scientists around the world use man-made nesting boxes to encourage breeding.

Young parrots will not venture from their nest until they are sure it is safe.

The African grey parrot is known for its uncanny ability to echo human speech.

Some of the most exciting parrot studies center on uncovering the mysteries of parrot mimicry. One of the most famous talking parrots was Alex, an African grey parrot that was purchased from a Chicago pet store in 1977 by scientist Irene Pepperberg. Between 1977 and 2007, when Alex died at the age of 31, Pepperberg taught Alex more than 100 words, including how to ask for objects and food. He could identify numbers and colors, which led Pepperberg to believe that Alex could comprehend the instructions she gave him. For many years, it was thought that parrots could only mimic sounds they hear without understanding what they are saying.

So how do parrots talk? Scientists have discovered that the birds use their strong tongue muscles to create variations in speech. Previously, it was thought that only humans had that ability. Parrots may actually be observing humans talk and imitating their tongue and mouth movements, just as a human baby would.

One of the biggest policy changes regarding parrots is occurring in the wild bird pet trade. Today, the world community realizes that the more wild parrots are taken from their natural habitat, the more rapidly wild

The African grey parrot has a very fast wing beat, flapping its wings 300 beats per minute (five times per second)!

Whether they are in flight (above) or at rest (opposite), parrots continue to awe people with their beauty.

populations decrease. In 2007, the European Union (EU) permanently banned the importation of wild birds into member countries. This was designed to stop the spread of infectious diseases, including the bird flu. Parrot conservationists applauded the measure, as this meant that an estimated four million birds would remain in the wild and not be sold as pets. Before the ban was implemented, EU countries made up a large percentage of the world's market for wild birds, importing two million each year from continents such as Africa and South America.

Despite such measures against illegal trade, it still exists. Parrots are smuggled into countries for sale, or importers use false documentation. The birds are taken to shipping centers in countries where export rules are more relaxed. U.S. Fish and Wildlife Service officials estimate that 20,000 birds are smuggled into the U.S. from Mexico each year.

But all of the recent research and new laws offer good news for parrots and people who enjoy them. The relationship between the birds and humans is thousands of years old, and the fascination with parrots is not likely to decrease. If people can help guard against further

destruction of parrot habitat, the bird's populations are sure
to stay steady—and possibly even increase—in years to
come. Scientists, researchers, and bird lovers everywhere
would love nothing more than to see that happen.

ANIMAL TALE: WHY PARROTS ONLY REPEAT THE WORDS OF HUMANS

Parrots have played a role in shaping many cultures around the world, from the ancient Mayans' macaws in Mexico to the Australians' 50 species of parrot today. They have always been an object of adoration, for their beautiful feathers, and an object of curiosity, for their ability to "talk." The following story, from a 1902 work called *The Book of Nature Myths*, provides one explanation for why parrots repeat the words of others.

When the earth was newly created, all birds could speak and carry on conversations with humans. In one village, there lived a well-loved parrot who always told the truth. But the parrot lived with a murderous thief, and one night it saw the man kill another man's ox and hide the body.

When the ox's owner searched the village for his animal, he asked the thief if he had seen the ox.

"No, I have not seen it," the man lied.

"Do you tell the truth?" the ox's owner asked.

"Yes, I am telling the truth. I have not seen your ox," said the thief.

To help find the ox, villagers suggested they ask the parrot, the bird of truth.

"Parrot, does this man tell the truth?" asked the ox's owner. "Has he not seen the ox?"

The parrot replied, "This man lies. I saw him kill the ox and hide the body."

The villagers and the ox's owner vowed to punish the thief the next day. Meanwhile, the thief devised a way to escape his dire situation.

When night came, the thief snuck up on the

parrot and covered it with a large jar. He placed
a blanket over the jar, poured water on it, and
banged upon it with a wooden spoon. He did this
for half the night, then went to bed.

When the villagers came for the thief the next
morning, the thief asked, "Why do you say it is I
who killed the ox?"

One man replied, "The bird said so, and the
bird always tells the truth."

"The bird of truth!" exclaimed the thief. "He
does not even know what happened last night.
Why don't you ask him if the moon was shining?"

"Was the moon out last night?" asked one
man, knowing full well it had been a clear,
cloudless night.

"No," said the parrot. "There was a great
storm, with much rain and thunder. I didn't see
the moon at all."

There was much chattering among the
villagers. A man cried out, "Why, this bird is lying!
He doesn't tell the truth after all."

The villagers forced the parrot out of the
village, and he went to live in the woods.

The parrot was very sad. He found a
mockingbird and told him what had happened.

"Why don't you just repeat the words of
man, instead of saying your own words?" the
mockingbird asked. "If you say what they say, they
will think you are a clever and smart bird."

"Yes, that's a good idea," the parrot said.
"That way, I would not be punished for telling
the truth. From now on, I will only repeat the
words of others."

GLOSSARY

aviaries – large, enclosed facilities in which birds are kept and allowed to fly freely within the confines

camouflage – the ability to hide, due to coloring or markings that blend in with a given environment

elegy – a poem of mourning, reflecting upon the death of someone or something

feral – an untamed animal that lives in the wild or one that leaves domestication and returns to the wild

hieroglyphics – a system of writing consisting of pictures and symbols that was used by ancient Egyptians

incubates – keeps an egg warm and protected until it is time for a chick to emerge

mandible – the jaw; in birds and insects, the mandible refers to both upper and lower jaw

mimic – to imitate a word or sound

plumage – the distinctive outer feathers on a bird

preen – to smooth or clean feathers with the bill

regurgitated – the partially digested food brought back up from an animal's stomach

roosts – trees with branches where birds sleep and rest

staggered – arranged in an orderly fashion

SELECTED BIBLIOGRAPHY

The Alex Foundation. "Alex Foundation Research." The Alex Foundation. http://www.alexfoundation.org/.

Collar, N. J. "Family Psittacidae (Parrots)." In *Handbook of the Birds of the World*, edited by J. del Hoyo, A. Elliott, and J. Sargatal, 280–339. Barcelona: Lynx Edicions, 1997.

Forshaw, Joseph Michael. *Parrots of the World: An Identification Guide*. Princeton, N.J.: Princeton University Press, 2006.

Horton, Casey. *Endangered Parrots*. New York: Benchmark Books, 1996.

Lantermann, Werner. *The New Parrot Handbook*. Woodbury, N.Y.: Barron's, 1985.

Low, Rosemary. *The Complete Book of Parrots*. New York: Barron's, 1988.

The scarlet and blue and gold macaws are 2 of about 18 macaw species native to the Americas.

INDEX